Original title:
Snowbound Skies

Author: Eliora Lumiste
ISBN HARDBACK: 978-9916-79-318-3
ISBN PAPERBACK: 978-9916-79-319-0
ISBN EBOOK: 978-9916-79-320-6

Secrets Frozen in Air

Whispers dance on frosty breath,
Echoes trapped in winter's depth.
Shadows glide on icy trails,
Silent stories held in gales.

Crystals spark in pale moonlight,
Secrets wrapped in winter's night.
Nature breathes a frozen sigh,
Truths concealed as time slips by.

Lullabies of the Winter Moon

Silver beams on sleeping trees,
Winter's hush brings gentle ease.
Lullabies that softly drift,
Melodies from time's great gift.

Cold winds sing a tender tune,
Cradled by the winter moon.
Dreams entwined in crystal white,
Whispers soft as stars ignite.

Icicles and Starry Nights

Icicles dangle, pure and bright,
Glistening under starlit night.
Frozen beauty, nature’s art,
A canvas forged from winter's heart.

Quiet moments, silence deep,
Beneath the stars, the world in sleep.
Gaze upwards, let your spirit soar,
In the magic we can't ignore.

A Canvas of Glimmering Silence

Snowflakes fall, a gentle grace,
Painting dreams in purest space.
Whispers lost in snowy hush,
Timeless moments wrapped in blush.

Blankets soft, embrace the chill,
Nature's palette, calm and still.
Each flake tells a tale untold,
In the silence, hearts unfold.

Ethereal Frost Beneath the Milky Way

A glimmer soft on silver fields,
Stars whisper secrets, time yields.
Frosted breath in the night air,
Dreams unfold with gentle care.

Echoes dance on shimmering light,
Chasing shadows, bidding goodnight.
The cosmos wraps us in its grace,
In this vast and endless space.

A Choreography of Ice and Stars

Twinkling diamonds on silken ice,
Each flake a moment, pure and precise.
They twirl and swirl in silent speech,
A ballet only night can teach.

Beneath the gaze of the glowing moon,
Nature's whispers form a tune.
Frosty tendrils connect our souls,
In this dance, the universe unfolds.

Glimmering Nightfall

As dusk embraces the waiting trees,
The stars emerge with gentle ease.
A tapestry of shimmering light,
Cloaks the world in tranquil night.

Soft shadows play where silence reigns,
Whispers glide through soft, cool strains.
The sky ignites, a canvas wide,
Nightfall sings; there's no need to hide.

The Hushed Waltz of Light

In the quiet where stars reside,
Light does waltz and softly glide.
Each twinkle tells a tale untold,
Of dreams and wishes, yet to unfold.

The moonlight spills on tranquil streams,
Weaving together the fabric of dreams.
Silence sways in the cool night air,
While the universe holds us with care.

Maple Branches Under Frost

Frosted leaves gleam bright,
In morning's gentle light.
Maple branches bend low,
Whispers of winter's glow.

A hush falls on the ground,
Nature's beauty profound.
Crystals twinkle and play,
As daylight fades away.

In silence, shadows dance,
A fleeting, cold romance.
Under skies painted gray,
Winter holds its sway.

The air is crisp and clear,
As stillness draws near.
Maples stand proud and tall,
Embracing it all.

Yet springs whispers arrive,
In hearts, hope will thrive.
A promise of new blooms,
As winter softly looms.

Dances with the Night Sky

Stars wink in serene grace,
The moonlight's warm embrace.
Whispers of the night call,
A dance for one and all.

Darkness swirls a gentle tune,
Underneath the silver moon.
Footsteps soft on the grass,
As momentous hours pass.

The constellations weave stories,
Of ancient dreams and glories.
In the cool, crisp night air,
Magic lingers everywhere.

Embers flicker in the breeze,
As shadows sway with ease.
Each star a twinkling light,
Guiding heart and soul's flight.

Dances with the night sky,
Where time seems to fly.
Together we shall soar,
Beyond the starlit shore.

Ephemeral Crystal Gardens

Glistening ice does gleam,
A cold yet vibrant dream.
Each flake a work of art,
A world set apart.

In gardens made of frost,
Beauty never lost.
Delicate shapes arise,
Under pale winter skies.

With every breath, we find,
Moments intertwined.
A touch of magic's grace,
In this enchanted place.

Soft whispers in the breeze,
Dance among the trees.
Fragile blooms, they unfold,
Stories of winter told.

Yet fleeting is their stay,
As sun will chase away.
But in the heart, they stay,
Ephemeral ballet.

Solstice Serenade

A time to gather near,
Voices soft, yet clear.
In the glow of candlelight,
We sing through the night.

Solstice brings its cheer,
A rhythm we hold dear.
Winter's chill, we embrace,
Finding warmth in this space.

Laughter dances around,
In love, we are found.
Stories shared by the flame,
Each heart sings the same.

Let the stars be our guide,
As the seasons collide.
A time for peace and joy,
Every girl, every boy.

Together we unite,
With spirits burning bright.
In this sacred parade,
We sing our solstice serenade.

Glimmers of the Frost Moon

A silver hue on sleeping pines,
Whispers soft in winter's breath.
Stars twinkle bright like distant signs,
Cold embraces life and death.

The night unfolds its silent tale,
With each breath a frosty kiss.
Dreamers dance in moonlit veil,
In this calm, we find our bliss.

Shadows stretch with gentle grace,
Glimmers spark in darkened skies.
Time slows down in this vast space,
Where secrets hide and beauty lies.

Underneath the frost's cool hold,
Nature rests, deep and serene.
In the stillness, stories told,
Of adventures yet unseen.

We gather warmth, share our dreams,
In the glow of winter's night.
With every hush the magic beams,
Beneath the frost moon's silver light.

Hibernation's Serenade

In the heart of winter's chill,
Creatures nestle, quiet, warm.
Time drifts slow, a gentle thrill,
Nature's pause, a soothing charm.

Snowflakes fall like whispered notes,
Cascading soft, a silken quilt.
In the stillness, life promotes,
Rest and peace, not guilt or guilt.

Branches bow with heavy frost,
Sheltering what the cold has sown.
In dreams, we wander, never lost,
Each heart beats softly, yet alone.

Sweet songs of slumber fill the air,
Echoes dance like fireflies' glow.
Wrapped in dreams without a care,
While outside, winter's winds will blow.

So let us bask in quiet night,
With fireside tales, warmth, and cheer.
In hibernation's soft delight,
We find the love that brings us near.

The Chill of Whispered Secrets

Beneath the stars, a silence grows,
A secret world in icy breath.
In shadows deep, where no one goes,
Whispers dance where echoes rest.

The frost unveils the midnight haze,
With every gust, tales intertwine.
Ancient trees in soft embrace,
Guarding histories, lost in time.

On frozen ground, the night reveals,
Stories trapped in crystal light.
Each whisper holds what truth conceals,
As winter shrouds the world in white.

Ghostly winds as secrets share,
A gentle touch, a sigh, a plea.
The chill wraps round with tender care,
In the stillness, we hear it flee.

So listen close, in peace abide,
For in the night, the answers gleam.
In whispered frost, our hearts confide,
On the edges of a dream.

Threads of Pale Light

In the dawn of winter's grace,
Fingers stretch to touch the sun.
Threads of pale light start to lace,
Awakening the day begun.

Each ray a gentle promise made,
Warming spirits frozen tight.
In the hush of morning's shade,
Dreams emerge from endless night.

Snowflakes shimmer in the glow,
Crafting beauty, pure and bright.
In this moment, time runs slow,
Wrapped in threads of pale, soft light.

Nature dances in the dawn,
Awakening from slumbered dreams.
As day breaks, the shadows yawn,
And every heart's alive, it seems.

So let the light weave through the trees,
Embrace the warmth, shed winter's chill.
With each moment, feel the breeze,
As threads of hope the world fulfill.

The Winter's Quiet Canvas

A blanket white lays on the ground,
Whispers of silence all around.
Trees are dressed in frosted lace,
Nature slows, in a gentle embrace.

Footprints trace a tale untold,
In the winter's breath, crisp and bold.
Shadows dance in fading light,
As day turns softly into night.

Birds nestle close, shelter from chill,
The world awaits, hushed and still.
Each breath clouds in the frosty air,
Winter's canvas, beyond compare.

Icicles hang like jewels so bright,
Glistening softly, pure delight.
Every corner a wonderland,
Nature's brush, a soft, steady hand.

As the moon rises, silver glow,
Winter's quiet, a gentle show.
With every flake that falls like rain,
Tomorrow's beauty calls again.

A Dance of Ice and Light

In the quiet night, stars gently gleam,
A dance of ice, a twilight dream.
Crystals sparkle, fragile and bright,
A symphony of shadows takes flight.

The frozen lake mirrors the sky,
As skaters glide, their spirits fly.
Laughter rings in the frosty air,
Joy of winter, beyond compare.

Snowflakes twirl like a ballet troupe,
Each one unique in the winter's loop.
Under the moon's soft, silvery ray,
Nature pauses, at the end of day.

Warmth in hearts, while the cold winds blow,
Holding tight to moments aglow.
Dancing together in soft twilight,
Creating magic, pure delight.

As dawn breaks, the colors unfold,
A promise of stories yet to be told.
In the dance of ice, we find our might,
Embracing winter's serene light.

Gleaming Pearls of Frost

Morning dew, a shimmer of grace,
Gleaming pearls in nature's embrace.
Whispers of frost on blushing blooms,
Every petal, a soft perfume.

As sunlight kisses the frosty ground,
Magic awakens, joy unbound.
Each droplet reflects a world anew,
The dance of diamonds, just for you.

Through tangled webs, glistening bright,
Nature’s jewels catch the light.
A tapestry woven with threads of frost,
In winter's grasp, beauty embossed.

Frigid air, yet warmth in our hearts,
A celebration in nature's arts.
With every breath, cold vapors rise,
Under the vast, endless skies.

Oh, how we cherish these moments rare,
Gleaming pearls in the crisp, clean air.
A fleeting glimpse of winter's grace,
In each frost's touch, a warm embrace.

Glistening Silhouettes

The sun dips low, casting long shades,
Glistening silhouettes in twilight fades.
Trees stand tall, mere shadows of night,
Sculpted in frost, a breathtaking sight.

In the amber glow, the world stands still,
Time unwinds under winter's chill.
Each branch a canvas, etched in ice,
Whispers of winter, cold and nice.

Footsteps crunch on the frosty ground,
Echoes of solitude all around.
In stillness, a silence so deep,
Awakening dreams from their sleep.

Stars begin to twinkle and play,
Guiding the night, holding shadows at bay.
With every breath, the air turns crisp,
In the dance of dusk, we quietly lisp.

Hold onto the beauty, fleeting and bright,
Glistening silhouettes in the night.
In the heart of winter, we find our spark,
Embracing the magic, lighting the dark.

Landscapes of Laced Pearl

Fields of silver, softly gleam,
Whispers dance in sunlight's beam.
Emerald dreams, the skies adorn,
In laced pearls, a world reborn.

Mountains rise with tranquil grace,
Clouds embrace the endless space.
Rivers weave through ancient stone,
Nature's love in every tone.

Petals fall like silent prayers,
Carpeted in life's own wares.
Glistening shores of morning dew,
Each moment feels forever new.

Winds of change, a gentle sigh,
Birds take flight, they soar and fly.
Beneath the sky, we find our way,
In landscapes bright, we long to stay.

Time stands still, a fleeting glance,
In this realm where hearts can dance.
With every breath, the world reveals,
The beauty that our spirit feels.

The Ice-Kissed Horizon

Frosted edges, stars so bright,
Whispers melt in winter's night.
The dawn breaks on an icy sea,
Where dreams wander, wild and free.

Glaciers glide through chill embrace,
Nature's art, a frozen grace.
Mountaintops with radiant glow,
Unlock secrets only cold can show.

Echoes linger in the breeze,
Snowflakes fall like whispered leaves.
Each breath, a shimmering delight,
A canvas clear in morning light.

Shadows dance on fields of white,
Creating tales of ancient might.
Time gets lost in stillness found,
While silence reigns, profound, unbound.

As horizons blend in hues,
The heart longs for the vibrant blues.
In the cold, we hold so near,
The warmth of love that draws us here.

Drifting with the Cold Currents

Sailing slowly through the mist,
Frozen waves, a gentle tryst.
Currents whisper secrets deep,
As the world around us sleeps.

A boat rocks on the frosty tides,
In this world where time abides.
Drifting softly, hearts align,
With the pulse of water's wine.

Starlit nights, the oceans hum,
Underneath the skies, we come.
Every wave, a tale untold,
In the chill, our fates unfold.

Beneath the surface, stories lie,
Soft and still, a lullaby.
Floating dreams of days gone by,
As we drift, the night draws nigh.

In these currents, lost and found,
Every heartbeat sings profound.
We'll embrace the cold around,
In frozen echoes, love is bound.

Flames Beneath the Frost

Amidst the chill, a fire glows,
Hidden warmth the heart bestows.
Underneath a blanket white,
Lies the pulse of hidden light.

Frosty air, a breath of steam,
Crackling embers, night's sweet dream.
Each flicker speaks of life within,
A dance of warmth, where hopes begin.

Snowflakes fall, a silent veil,
Yet the heart knows love won't pale.
Beneath the frost, the fire's code,
Ignites the path where spirits road.

In quiet moments, shadows play,
As flames keep coldness at bay.
With every spark, the warmth ignites,
Turning darkness into lights.

So let the frost come whisper low,
For under it, the flames still grow.
In the heart where love stays tossed,
We find our truth, though cold we're crossed.

Sledding Through Stardust

Under the winter's night sky,
Children gather, spirits high.
Sleds await on the glinting snow,
Laughter spills, their joy to show.

Gliding fast, they race the moon,
Stars above, a timeless tune.
With every turn, a whisper light,
Sledding dreams through frosty night.

Warm breaths rise in the chilly air,
Radiant smiles everywhere.
Adventures call on slopes so steep,
In stardust trails, moments keep.

Each descent, a fleeting flight,
Wrapped in blankets, cozy, tight.
Through the woven paths of snow,
Magic dances, hearts aglow.

As dawn creeps in, the world awakes,
Silence falls, a stillness breaks.
Yet memories spark, forever bright,
Sledding dreams on winter's night.

The Great White Embrace

Snowflakes tumbling from above,
Whispers soft like thoughts of love.
A blanket wraps the world anew,
Nature's grace in tranquil hue.

Trees wear coats of icy lace,
Branches bow in winter's grace.
Footprints mark the path we tread,
Hearts entwined, in warmth, we're led.

In the hush, all sounds are still,
Snow-capped hills, a magical thrill.
Together bound in frosty cheer,
Through the chill, no trace of fear.

Hot cocoa warms our time apart,
In the cold, we share our heart.
Each moment breathes the crisp, sweet air,
The great white embrace, beyond compare.

As evening falls, the sky ignites,
Colors blaze in winter nights.
Together still, our souls ignite,
In this embrace, we find our light.

Frosty Labyrinths

Winding paths of glimmering white,
Every turn a new delight.
Snowflakes dance like whispered dreams,
In the world, a soft gleam.

Crisp air swirls with sweet surprise,
Frosty breaths beneath the skies.
Steps lead on, where secrets hide,
In labyrinths where joys abide.

Children chase the shadows long,
In this chilly, playful song.
Every twist, a chance to learn,
With every laugh, the lanterns burn.

Nature's maze, a wonder found,
Footprints echo, magic bound.
Hold my hand as we explore,
In frosty realms forevermore.

As twilight falls, the stars will gleam,
In this frosty, wondrous dream.
Together paused, we catch our breath,
In labyrinths, we laugh at death.

Hushed Echoes of Winter

In the stillness, whispers sigh,
Snowflakes fall, they softly lie.
Nature's breath, a gentle hum,
Hushed echoes, the night has come.

Frosty air, a canvas vast,
Painting memories that will last.
Each flake tells a story clear,
In winter's grasp, we draw near.

Bare branches reach to touch the sky,
A ballet where shadows fly.
Wrapped in layers, warm, we stand,
At winter's gate, hand in hand.

Soft footsteps trace the white floor,
In silence, we find so much more.
Embraced by cold, yet warmed inside,
With nature's bliss, we cast aside.

As moonlight bathes the world in peace,
Hushed echoes, where worries cease.
In this quiet, we find our song,
Hushed echoes of winter, soft and strong.

The Stillness of Frigid Winds

In the hush of the night,
Whispers of frost take flight,
Silent echoes softly wane,
Cold wraps the earth in a chain.

Moonlight glimmers on the snow,
Where shadows dance, gentle and slow,
The world in slumber, pure and bright,
Frigid winds sing of the night.

Branches tremble, bare and still,
Soft sighs carried on the chill,
Nature holds her breath anew,
Underneath the sky of blue.

Footsteps muffled, lost in dream,
Frozen rivers wind and gleam,
Each moment hangs, time stands still,
Embracing winter's tranquil thrill.

Stars above, a distant cheer,
In the stillness, crystal clear,
In this winter's quiet grace,
We find warmth in nature's face.

Embrace of the Wintry Blue

In horizons draped in white,
The sky blends with the night,
Gentle flakes begin to fall,
Whispering secrets, winter's call.

Blue shadows stretch across the land,
Cold caress of nature's hand,
Frozen streams with beauty bind,
In their depths, peace we find.

As the world holds its tight grip,
Every breath a frosty sip,
Embrace the chill, welcome the hue,
In the silence, hearts renew.

Bare trees stand in quiet grace,
Against the wind, they find their place,
Nature's breath, so crisp and true,
Wraps the world in wintry blue.

Moments twirl like snowflakes bright,
Swirling softly, pure delight,
In this realm of cold and light,
Joy is found in winter's night.

The Icicle's Lament

Hanging low from eaves and beams,
Icicles weep with silver dreams,
In the grip of winter's breath,
Their softness speaks of nature's death.

Dripping slowly, crystal tears,
Whispers filled with ancient fears,
Each drop tells a tale of time,
A fleeting echo, soft and chime.

Brittle beauty, sharp and cold,
Holding secrets never told,
Fragile forms of art divine,
Reflecting light, a world benign.

As the sunlight warms the day,
These faithful sentinels decay,
Melting into pools of past,
Echoes of a season vast.

Yet in their fall, a song begins,
Of renewal found in loss, it spins,
From stalactites, life will break,
And winter's heart will start to wake.

Broken Stars in a Frozen World

Beneath a sky of endless night,
Stars lay scattered, dimmed in fright,
Frozen fields, a silver sea,
Holding dreams of what will be.

Each star twinkles, lost in space,
A distant memory, a trace,
Yet in their fall, they leave a spark,
Illuminating winter's dark.

Cold winds whisper soft and low,
Guiding hearts where starlights glow,
In the silence, hopes arise,
Broken stars tell no goodbyes.

Embers dance in icy breath,
Reminders bright, defying death,
In a frozen world so vast,
The light of love will ever last.

As dawn approaches, hues unfold,
A canvas brushed with threads of gold,
From broken stars, a story swirled,
Awakening a frozen world.

Winter's Ethereal Embrace

In the hush of falling snow,
A whisper of silence grows,
Trees adorned in frosty lace,
Nature's pure and gentle grace.

Crystals dance on frosty air,
Each flake a secret to share,
The world wrapped in a soft glow,
Where dreams and winter winds flow.

Footsteps crunch on icy ground,
A symphony of winter's sound,
Echoes of laughter resonate,
In this land, where stillness waits.

Night descends with stars aglow,
Beneath the moon's enchanting show,
Shadows flicker, glimmers bright,
In this realm of quiet light.

Hearts entwined in winter's arms,
Frosty breath and tender charms,
Together in this serene place,
We find love in winter's embrace.

Frost-Kissed Serenity

Morning light breaks through the mist,
Every surface softly kissed,
A world enveloped by quiet peace,
Where all worries seem to cease.

Trees wear coats of sparkling white,
Branches gleam in soft daylight,
The stillness wraps around so tight,
Frosted breath in pure delight.

Birds chirp gently, songs take flight,
In the air, a crisp delight,
Nature sighs in a whispered tone,
In this beauty, we find home.

Frozen ponds reflect the sky,
Glimmers where the shadows lie,
Ice transforms the mundane scene,
A tranquil vision, calm and clean.

Time slows down in winter's hold,
A soothing dream, both soft and bold,
In the heart of cold serenity,
We find warmth, our remedy.

Moonlight on Ice

Moonlight spills on frozen streams,
Casting light on midnight dreams,
Each shimmer tells a tale of night,
Wrapped in calm, a soft delight.

Whispers float on chilly air,
Echoes of secrets laid bare,
Stars twinkle in the velvet sky,
While shadows dance and spirits fly.

Footprints trace a winding path,
Through the stillness, peace will last,
As the world is draped in silver,
Every heart begins to quiver.

In the hush, our wishes soar,
Beneath the moon, we long for more,
Swirling thoughts like snowflakes fall,
In this moment, we are all.

The night embraces all in grace,
Breathless in this frozen space,
Together, lost in winter's spell,
In moonlight's dance, we find our tell.

Shadows in the Snow

Beneath the trees, shadows creep,
Whispers hide where silence sleeps,
In the snow, a crisp, white shroud,
Nature's beauty, serene and proud.

Footprints tell a silent tale,
Of fleeting dreams that softly sail,
The chill wraps tight around our skin,
As memories of warmth begin.

Nighttime falls with silver gleam,
A world transformed, a waking dream,
Stars above like lanterns glow,
Guiding us through paths of snow.

Embers of a fire's retreat,
Heartbeats echo, warm and sweet,
In the stillness, souls unite,
Bathed in shadows, pure delight.

Together we embrace the cold,
With every story gently told,
In this winter's quiet glow,
We find light in shadows' flow.

When the Sky Turns Velvet

As day surrenders, shadows creep,
The stars awaken, the world in sleep.
Whispers of night begin to play,
When the sky turns velvet, night holds sway.

The moon ascends, a silver glow,
Casting dreams on fields below.
A tranquil hush, the crickets call,
In the velvet sky, we feel so small.

The Milky Way, a silk-threaded seam,
Stitches together each fading dream.
In this vastness, we lose our plight,
When the sky turns velvet, hearts take flight.

Beneath the stars, we share our fears,
In the stillness, we shed our tears.
The velvet night, a soft embrace,
Where time suspends, we find our place.

As dawn approaches, colors blend,
A fleeting moment, night must end.
Yet in our hearts, this truth shall stay,
When the sky turns velvet, dreams don't fade away.

Clouds of Sugar Crystal

In the morning light, a gentle sight,
Clouds of sugar crystal take their flight.
Fragile forms on a canvas so wide,
Dancing softly with the breeze as their guide.

With every hue, they shift and sway,
Bright whispers of joy in celestial play.
They paint the skies, a delightful scene,
Clouds of sugar crystal, so sweet, serene.

As the sun sets, they catch ablaze,
A blush of colors, a fiery haze.
Moments like these, we wish to hold,
Clouds of sugar crystal, stories untold.

The twilight deepens, their magic lingers,
Framed by stars dancing on delicate fingers.
A fleeting wonder, the night will take,
But in our hearts, these moments awake.

Gone with the night, yet not in vain,
Their beauty remains like a soft refrain.
In dreams, we'll chase them, as shadows swirl,
Clouds of sugar crystal, where wonders unfurl.

The Frozen Embrace of Twilight

In the hush of dusk, where shadows grow,
The frozen embrace of twilight begins to show.
A tender stillness, the world holds breath,
As colors blend in the dance of death.

Cool winds whisper through branches bare,
With every gust, secrets in the air.
A palette of blue, gold and gray,
In the frozen embrace, night claims the day.

The stars peek out, like diamonds bright,
Winking softly in the coming night.
In this frozen hour, we pause and see,
The beauty found in tranquility.

As darkness settles, the heart feels peace,
In the frozen embrace, all troubles cease.
A fleeting moment, yet deeply it lingers,
Captured forever in memory's fingers.

In twilight's grasp, we find our way,
With hope reborn as night leads the day.
The frozen embrace, a gentle sigh,
Wrapped in wonder as the world spins by.

Painted in Winter's Breath

With every flake that twirls and glides,
The world transforms as softness hides.
A canvas pure, untouched by strife,
Painted in winter's breath, full of life.

Trees wear coats of glistening white,
As snowflakes dance beneath the light.
Each branch adorned, a sparkle bright,
In this chilly realm, everything feels right.

Crisp air whispers secrets to the ear,
A chilling beauty that draws us near.
In the quiet hush, we learn to see,
How winter's breath shapes our glee.

Footsteps crunch on paths long gone,
Memories formed as season’s song,
In the stillness, the world stands still,
Painted in winter’s breath, hearts we fill.

With cozy fires and laughter's glow,
We gather close as the winds blow.
In this embrace of frost and cheer,
Winter’s breath brings us all near.

The Tranquil Echo of Cold

In the stillness of the night,
Whispers of frost take flight.
Shadows dance on silent ground,
Nature’s peace in echoes found.

Moonlight glistens on the trees,
A gentle sigh in the breeze.
Each breath a tale softly told,
In the tranquil echo of cold.

Footsteps crunch on winter's breath,
A journey stretched, a dance with death.
Stars above, a gleaming sight,
Wrapped in the cloak of quiet night.

The world asleep, embraced in chill,
Covered deep, the heart can feel.
Time slows down, the hours pass,
In crystal silence, moments last.

As dawn arrives, a soft blush spread,
Golden rays where shadows tread.
Cold fades gently, warmth awakes,
In the echo, peace still quakes.

Luminous Frost Upon the Earth

A shimmer spreads across the land,
Frosted petals like fine sand.
Glowing softly in morning light,
Nature's canvas, pure and bright.

Crystals form on every leaf,
A scene that stirs the heart's belief.
Beneath the sun, a sparkling show,
Winter's charm in frosted glow.

Each step whispers in the hush,
Time pauses, amidst the rush.
Luminous frost, a fleeting grace,
Holds the world in a gentle embrace.

As shadows lengthen, colors blend,
A twilight kiss, the day will end.
Stars emerge, to dance above,
In the night, warmth is love.

Tomorrow brings more glistening dew,
Each dawn anew, a breath of hue.
Luminous frost, here to impart,
Beauty woven in the heart.

Celestial Reflections in Ice

In the stillness, moments freeze,
Mirrored skies where dreams can tease.
Frozen lakes, a glassy shield,
Celestial wonders are revealed.

Stars like diamonds twinkle bright,
Glimmering soft in the velvet night.
Each reflection holds its light,
In the quiet, pure delight.

Whispers echo across the face,
Time stands still; a sacred space.
Nature's art, a crafted sigh,
Where earth and heaven seem to lie.

Every breath, a fragile sound,
Echoes of love deeply found.
Celestial reflections unfold,
Stories of warmth in the cold.

As dawn arrives, shadows lift,
A symphony, the day’s new gift.
Ice melts softly in morning's grace,
Revealing beauty, a warm embrace.

Threads of Chill

Beneath the sky of silver hue,
Threads of chill weave life anew.
Whispers ride on winter's air,
A tapestry, both bright and rare.

Glimmers dance on frosted ground,
Nature's quilt, a playful sound.
Each gust spins a tale untold,
In the fabric of the cold.

Horizon blushes with the dawn,
Chill retreats, yet lingers on.
Threads of light begin to fray,
Winter's thread transforms the day.

Footprints mark the path we take,
In the chill, our hearts awake.
Woven dreams in twilight's lace,
Finding warmth in winter's grace.

As twilight casts its gentle shade,
Threads of chill will never fade.
In every heartbeat, every breath,
A song of life, the dance with death.

Echoes of the Frozen Dawn

In the quiet woods, whispers freeze,
Trees bow down, caught in the breeze.
Footsteps crunch on the frosty ground,
Echoes of silence, profound and round.

Morning light kisses the snow-white crest,
A world awakes, in its winter vest.
Soft shadows dance in the first sunlight,
Echoes remain in the shimmering white.

Birds take flight in the chilly air,
Bright against blue, a fleeting flare.
Their songs resonate, sweet and clear,
In the frozen dawn, they draw near.

Nature holds its breath so still,
Each breath of frost is a gentle thrill.
With every heartbeat, a story unfolds,
In echoes of dawn, the winter holds.

The sun rises slow, a golden balm,
Awakening earth with a soothing calm.
Each echo lingers, a soft refrain,
In the frozen dawn, we feel the gain.

The Celestial Chill Above

Stars twinkle brightly in the deep night,
Each a whisper, a guiding light.
The moon hangs low, a silver sphere,
Casting dreams on the world so dear.

Beneath the vast and endless skies,
The chill embraces, where silence lies.
Galaxies dance in a cosmic sway,
A celestial chill that holds sway.

Winds carry tales from far-off lands,
Through icy realms, where time withstands.
The universe hums a timeless tune,
Beneath the stars and the watchful moon.

Snowflakes drift like thoughts on the breeze,
Soft as secrets, they land with ease.
A wonder of nature, this peaceful glade,
In the celestial chill, our fears fade.

Each night offers a canvas anew,
With glimmers of hope in shades of blue.
The chill above sings an ancient song,
In the cosmos vast, we all belong.

Glacial Veils and Twinkling Stars

Underneath glacial veils so bright,
Sparkling diamonds in the moonlight.
Nature’s canvas flows, serene and pure,
Hidden treasures that none can cure.

Twinkling stars adorn the night’s cloak,
Each a story, a silent joke.
Glacial whispers float in the air,
Secrets of earth, beyond compare.

Crystals form where shadows play,
In the icy breath of a winter's day.
The night sky stitches dreams with care,
As glacial veils float everywhere.

Silent wonders, as soft as snow,
In glacial realms where soft winds blow.
Each twinkle a promise, deeply cast,
In the arms of night, our hearts hold fast.

Together in this frozen land,
With glacial veils and stars at hand.
We dance in wonder, fearless and free,
In the cosmic chill, just you and me.

When the World Sleeps White

When the world sleeps beneath soft snow,
A blanket of silence, moonlit glow.
Shadows stretch long, soft and wide,
In the hush of night, where dreams reside.

Frosty whispers through branches flow,
Nature’s breath, gentle and low.
In the stillness, magic unfolds,
A tale of winter, patiently told.

Houses glow with warmth inside,
As outside freezes, hopes collide.
Each flake that falls brings a new start,
Painting the earth, a work of art.

Stars peek through in the chilly air,
Their twinkling eyes watch without a care.
The world holds its breath in the deep of night,
Wrapped in tranquility, pure and white.

Awake to morning's gentle grace,
The world transformed, a soft embrace.
When the world sleeps, dreams take flight,
In a blanket of snow, pure and bright.

The Silent Blanket

Softly falls the quiet snow,
A gentle hush, the world in tow.
Each flake a whisper, light and mild,
Nature wrapped in dreams beguiled.

Bare branches wear their crystal crowns,
The earth adorned in quiet gowns.
Footprints fade like fleeting time,
In this stillness, echoes rhyme.

The moonlight dances on the ground,
Creating magic all around.
A silent blanket soft and wide,
Holds the warmth of dreams inside.

Within this peace, reflections glow,
On winter's stage, a tranquil show.
The heart finds solace in the night,
Wrapped in the snow's purest light.

Frosted Horizons

Beyond the fields, where shadows play,
A frosted touch transforms the day.
The sun casts sparkles on the frost,
In every breath, a moment lost.

Horizon whispers promises bright,
Painting the morn with hues of light.
While nature holds her breath so still,
Frosted dreams upon the hill.

The chill of air, a crisp embrace,
Each step revealing winter's grace.
With every glance, the world anew,
In frosted views, the heart breaks through.

Clouds trail softly, drifting low,
As distant echoes swell and grow.
Frosted horizons stretch so wide,
Where earth and sky in beauty bide.

Glacial Reverie

Upon the peaks where silence reigns,
A glacial dream in shadowed chains.
Time stands still in icy breath,
Nature's calm, a dance with death.

Crystals gleam in twilight's grasp,
Each moment lingers, soft and fast.
Whispers carried on the breeze,
A tapestry of frozen ease.

Mountains loom with ancient pride,
Guardians where the spirits bide.
In their shadows, tales unfold,
Of glacial years and dreams of gold.

A reverie in shades of blue,
Where skies embrace the mountains too.
In stillness found, a world preserved,
In glacial beauty, souls are served.

Whispering Clouds of White

Whispering clouds drift soft and slow,
Draped in a mist of winter's glow.
They carry tales from far away,
In shades of gray and hints of play.

Beneath their dance, the world feels light,
As shadows weave in soft twilight.
Each breath a whisper on the breeze,
Floating dreams among the trees.

The sky awash with gentle hues,
A canvas painted with winter's blues.
As clouds embrace the earth so near,
They cradle secrets, hush and clear.

Through drifting veils of cotton white,
The heart finds warmth in fleeting light.
In every sigh, a promise looms,
Of whispering clouds and peaceful blooms.

Poetry of the Silent Storm

Whispers of wind through the night,
Gentle shadows take their flight.
Clouds gather with a silent grace,
Nature holds a breathless space.

Lightning flickers, a fleeting glance,
In darkness, shadows start to dance.
Raindrops fall like soft-spun dreams,
Creating rivers, crafting streams.

Thunder rumbles, a distant drum,
The heart's pulse begins to hum.
Silence speaks in a thunderous way,
A symphony in shades of gray.

Branches sway, a tender sigh,
Under the watchful stormy sky.
In the storm, all feels alive,
In chaos, beauty seeks to thrive.

As clouds part and the sun breaks through,
A softer world, with colors anew.
In the calm that follows night,
Poetry blooms in morning’s light.

Crystalline Reverie

Glistening flakes fall from above,
Each a whisper of winter love.
Blanketing earth in hues so bright,
A shimmering world, pure delight.

Icicles hang like crystal tears,
Drawing laughter, drowning fears.
In this realm of frozen dreams,
Light dances through with silver beams.

Trees clad in robes of icy lace,
Stand tall, they hold a prayerful grace.
Beneath the weight, they bow and bend,
In silent reverie that won’t end.

Footsteps crunch on powdery ground,
In winter's embrace, peace is found.
Every breath a cloud in the air,
Moments linger, sweet and rare.

When dusk falls with a gentle sigh,
Stars emerge in the velvet sky.
In this crystalline reverie,
Magic weaves through eternity.

Ethereal Echoes in the Cold

Whispers ride the frozen breeze,
Carried far beyond the trees.
Ghostly echoes, soft and clear,
Call out secrets for all to hear.

Moonlight bathes the tranquil night,
Casting shadows bathed in light.
A serenade of winds so bold,
Sings eternal tales of cold.

Each flake that falls tells a story,
Of winter's fleeting, fleeting glory.
Underneath the silence deep,
The heart of winter yearns to weep.

Crystals sparkle in the glow,
Reflecting dreams of long ago.
In this frozen, ethereal show,
Time stands still, and thoughts can flow.

As dawn breaks with a soft embrace,
Echoes fade without a trace.
Yet in the cold, the whispers stay,
An echo’s song will not decay.

The Shattered Winter's Light

A fractured dawn across the snow,
Light spills softly, a gentle glow.
Shadows stretch with the morn's delight,
Daybreak blooms in colors bright.

Brittle branches, ice entwined,
Each sparkle warms the heart and mind.
In the stillness, silence shrinks,
While winter's beauty softly winks.

Melting snowdrops, a tender sigh,
Life awakens, winter bids goodbye.
Crystals fall with a tinkling sound,
In their shatter, new life is found.

A tapestry of frost and sun,
In every shard, a thread begun.
Moments linger, fate's soft embrace,
In shattered light, we find our place.

As evening whispers softly low,
The sky ignites with amber glow.
In the twilight, hearts ignite,
Flickering flames in the winter's night.

Ethereal Echoes on Silent Nights

Whispers float on moonlit air,
Stars twinkle in the velvet dark.
Softly dreams begin to share,
As shadows dance with whispered spark.

Among the trees, a secret calls,
Echoes of a timeless plea.
Through the night the silence sprawls,
In the hush, the heart beats free.

Luna smiles, the world aglow,
Guiding footsteps on the way.
In the stillness, peace will grow,
Cradling thoughts as night turns gray.

Every glance, a tale unfolds,
In the quiet, stories bloom.
Memories wrapped in silver folds,
In the dark, there's much to room.

Ethereal dreams take their flight,
As night's embrace pulls hearts close.
In the canvas of soft light,
We find solace, pure as prose.

The Gallery of Frozen Echoes

Framed in ice, time stands still,
A gallery of moments paused.
Captured whispers, frozen thrill,
In the stillness, beauty's caused.

Glistening snowflakes gently land,
Each unique, a fleeting grace.
Nature's art, a sculptor’s hand,
Crafting wonders in this space.

Footprints mark the path once tread,
Stories linger in the air.
Every silence softly said,
Haunting echoes, everywhere.

Pine trees dressed in frosted white,
Guardians of the frozen scene.
Underneath the starry night,
Whispers weave through evergreen.

In this gallery, time unwinds,
Each encounter a new refrain.
Amidst the still, our hearts can find,
Life’s sweet ache in joy and pain.

Captured Crystals in Twilight

Twilight hangs in hues so bold,
As daylight fades and night appears,
Crystals glisten, stories told,
In shadows, laughter spills with tears.

Fragments of a day now gone,
Reflecting on the fading light.
In the hush, the dreams are drawn,
Captured moments, taking flight.

Silhouettes of distant trees,
Swaying gently in the breeze.
Nature's whispers, soft as pleas,
In twilight's grasp, we find our ease.

Every star begins to gleam,
Painting skies with hopes anew.
In this twilight, we will dream,
Embracing all that is true.

Crystals dance in fading hue,
A symphony of night’s embrace.
Captured moments, ours to view,
In twilight's arms, we find our place.

A Tapestry of White Hues

Frosted whispers fill the air,
A tapestry of crystal white.
Nature's wonder, pure and rare,
Wrapping earth in soft delight.

Each flake falls like gentle grace,
Covering all in a calming shroud.
In this winter's warm embrace,
Silent beauty, bright and proud.

Branches bow with burdens light,
Snowflakes dance, a fleeting fling.
Every moment shines so bright,
In this world, we hear it sing.

Starlit nights and days so gray,
In this canvas, we unite.
Through the frost, we find our way,
Guided by the purest light.

A tapestry of whispers spun,
In each corner, magic brewed.
With every breath, a heart is won,
In white hues, our spirits renewed.

The Chill of Dusk

The sun retreats, a weary light,
As shadows stretch in fading sight.
Whispers of night begin to rise,
Beneath the darkening skies.

A breeze slips through the swaying trees,
Bringing with it a chill, a tease.
The world, now hushed, holds its breath,
In stillness, it dances with death.

Colors melt, a canvas gray,
Echoes of warmth begin to stray.
The twilight wraps in soft embrace,
As night unfurls its velvet lace.

Stars appear, a scattered glow,
Illuminating the paths below.
With every blink, a story told,
In the quiet, both vivid and bold.

The chill of dusk, a gentle call,
Where dreams awaken, shadows fall.
In the twilight, we find our way,
Through the silence of end of day.

Shimmering Nightfall

The moon ascends, a silver queen,
Casting light on fields of green.
A shimmering veil drapes the land,
Guiding dreams with a gentle hand.

Stars twinkle like whispers of lore,
Each a secret, forevermore.
The night unfolds, a promise kept,
In its embrace, the world has slept.

Cool air dances with fragrant blooms,
As darkness wraps in quiet rooms.
Shadows play on the cobbled streets,
Where night and day softly meet.

Reflections glimmer on the lake,
As ripples form in their wake.
The serenade of crickets sings,
Echoed by the flutter of wings.

In shimmering nightfall, we roam,
Wandering far from our earthly home.
A tapestry woven of light and night,
In dreams we soar, in silence, take flight.

A Tapestry of Frost

Morning breaks, a soft embrace,
With frost that paints the world in grace.
Delicate crystals on each branch,
Nature dons her wintry stance.

The ground is still, a carpet white,
Reflecting shards of early light.
Each breath a cloud, we linger slow,
In this realm where chill winds blow.

Glistening fields, a wondrous sight,
Awakening to the day's first light.
Whispers of ice greet the dawn,
As nature's beauty lingers on.

Lone trees stretch against the sky,
Guardians of secrets, you and I.
In silent awe, we witness here,
A tapestry of frost so clear.

As sunlight warms the frozen ground,
The beauty shifts, yet still is found.
In every flake, a story lies,
A moment captured, time defies.

Beyond the Icy Veil

In shadows deep, the secrets dwell,
Beyond the icy veil, we tell.
A land where whispers softly sing,
Of frost-kissed dreams and wintry spring.

Mountains loom, their peaks frost-clad,
Guardians of tales, both good and bad.
Through windswept paths, our footsteps trace,
The echoes of a cold embrace.

Silver rivers in silence flow,
Beneath the ice, the heartbeats grow.
Life persists in hidden streams,
Awakening the muted dreams.

In the twilight, spirits dance,
Encased in magic, they take a chance.
To slip through ice, to rise and sail,
To find the world beyond the veil.

With each breath, the cold we face,
Is but a veil, a sweet embrace.
For beyond that chill, warmth will bloom,
A place where life can still resume.

Shadows in Frosted Light

Amidst the glow of pale moon's beam,
Shadows dance in a silver dream.
Frosty whispers trace the night,
Stars above in quiet flight.

The trees stand tall, their branches bare,
Cloaked in white, a crystal care.
Footprints crunch on snowy grounds,
Nature's hush in soft surrounds.

Glimmers play on surfaces slick,
Winter's breath, a gentle trick.
Softly gliding, silent grace,
In this beauty, we embrace.

Through the chill, a warmth ignites,
Hearts entwined on frosty nights.
In these shadows, love can thrive,
Together, we feel so alive.

When dawn awakes the world anew,
Frosted light bursts into view.
Hope unfurls like morning's glow,
In shadows cast, our spirits flow.

Celestial Drift of Winter's Breath

In the stillness of the night,
Winter's breath takes its flight.
Softly drifting, snowflakes fall,
Nature's whisper, a gentle call.

Underneath the starry skies,
Celestial wonders catch our eyes.
Frozen dreams in the cold air,
Beauty lingers everywhere.

The silence wraps the world so tight,
In the arms of soft moonlight.
Every flake a tale retold,
In these moments, hearts unfold.

Winds that carry winter's grace,
Guiding us to a tranquil place.
In this calm, our spirits lift,
Bearing witness to the gift.

As dawn arrives, the light aligns,
Painting shadows with thin lines.
In the drift, we find our peace,
In winter's breath, sweet release.

The Serene Touch of Cold

Veils of frost on windowpanes,
Whispers echo, soft refrains.
The world adorned in sparkling white,
The serene touch of cold invites.

Each breath curls into misty air,
Fleeting moments beyond compare.
Quiet streets in slumber's hold,
Wrapped in blankets, night unfolds.

Burdened trees wear coats of frost,
Nature's beauty, never lost.
In every flake, a memory waits,
Tales of wonder, whispered fates.

Laughter twinkles like stars above,
Sharing warmth, a dance of love.
Through the chill, we find the light,
In simple joys that feel just right.

Embrace the cold, let spirits soar,
In winter's grasp, there's so much more.
The serene touch, together we find,
A lasting bond, forever entwined.

Whispers in the Winter Breeze

Whispers flutter on the breeze,
Carried softly through the trees.
In the hush, the world dissolves,
Winter's secrets gently solve.

Cascades of white blanket the ground,
Through the silence, joy is found.
Each breath a puff of gentle chill,
Filling hearts with peaceful thrill.

The horizon glows in muted hues,
Painting skies with icy blues.
Footsteps trace a pathway bright,
In winter’s calm, we find our light.

Stories whispered, stars align,
In this moment, love we find.
Frozen kisses on cheeks so red,
Whispers linger, softly said.

As evening falls and shadows play,
We hold on tight, we find our way.
Through the chill, our spirits soar,
In the winter's breeze, we want for more.

Crystal Shrouds Above

In twilight's glow, they gleam so bright,
A cloak of ice, a pure delight.
Between the trees, they softly dance,
A fleeting glimpse, a whispered chance.

The world below in silence waits,
While crystal shrouds adorn the gates.
A fragile world, both cold and fair,
Beneath the weight of winter's care.

Each breath a cloud, the air so thin,
The magic flows, where dreams begin.
And in this realm, the heart takes flight,
With crystal shrouds, we chase the night.

The stars above, a silent choir,
Their light a balm, a warming fire.
No words are needed, just the light,
Of crystal shrouds that shine so bright.

We walk in wonder, hand in hand,
Through frozen paths, across this land.
For in this moment, we are free,
With crystal shrouds, just you and me.

A Tundra of Stars

In the hush of night, the tundra breathes,
A blanket soft, the world it weaves.
Stars scatter wide, like diamonds tossed,
In velvet skies where dreams are lost.

Each glimmer holds a tale untold,
Of ancient nights and hearts so bold.
The frostbit air, a gentle kiss,
In this vast space, we find our bliss.

Through icy winds, we make our way,
With whispered hopes, we dare to sway.
The universe, a canvas bright,
We paint our dreams in silver light.

In shadows deep, our spirits soar,
A tundra vast, yet we implore.
For every star that lights the skies,
Reminds us of our endless ties.

In stillness found, we learn to trust,
The night, the stars, the frozen dust.
Together here, we find our light,
In this tundra of stars, pure and bright.

Time Slows Under the Frost

Beneath the frost, time gently wanes,
In stillness bound, the heart remains.
Each crystal flake that falls so slow,
Creates a world where memories flow.

The icy breath of winter's spell,
In every hush, a story to tell.
As shadows stretch, and daylight leaves,
The night conceals what the heart believes.

The clock unwinds, its hands at rest,
In frozen dreams, we find our quest.
With every heartbeat, moments cling,
As time, like frost, begins to sing.

In quiet fields where sorrows fade,
We weave a path through ice and shade.
Embracing stillness, we find our worth,
In these serene, enchanted hearths.

So let the winter's chill enfold,
As stories whispered softly unfold.
For in this realm, where all is lost,
We find our peace, 'neath time's soft frost.

Spheres of Winterlight

In quiet glades, where shadows play,
The spheres of light lead us away.
They twirl and spin, like dreams in flight,
Illuminating the cold, dark night.

Each orb a glow of tender grace,
A beacon bright in this vast space.
They guide our steps on frozen ground,
With whispers soft, their magic found.

Through frosted trees, their secrets gleam,
In every flicker, a waking dream.
For winter's touch can't dim their spark,
With spheres of light, we chase the dark.

In every breath, the chill runs deep,
Yet in these lights, we dare to leap.
For hope ignites in the coldest hours,
Through spheres of winterlight, we flower.

So let us dance in this enchanted glow,
With hearts aflame against the snow.
Together, here, we find our way,
Through spheres of light, come what may.

Embers Beneath the Iced Veil

In shadows deep, the embers glow,
Silent warmth in a world of snow.
Beneath the chill, a firely breath,
Whispers of life beyond the death.

Branches twinkle, adorned in frost,
Echoes of beauty, never lost.
The heart beats soft, hidden from sight,
A dance of sparks in the cold night.

Breath of winter, a gentle sigh,
Stars are cloaked in a velvet sky.
Yet beneath the ice, a spark ignites,
A promise of spring in the frozen nights.

Snowflakes whisper, tales of old,
Of warmth and fire, and hearts of gold.
Each crunch beneath, a hidden song,
Of embers waiting, where they belong.

So let the night, in silence fall,
For life endures through the icy call.
Embers flicker, a faint embrace,
In the frozen world, warmth finds its place.

Journey Through Frozen Whispers

Through the woods, a path unfolds,
Frozen whispers, muffled and bold.
Each step reveals a story untold,
In shimmering frost, the silence molds.

Echoes dance on the icy ground,
Nature's voice, both soft and profound.
A tapestry woven in frosty threads,
Carrying secrets of those who tread.

Beneath the frost, life stirs and dreams,
In the hush, where the moonlight beams.
Each breath a spark, aflame with desire,
Journey ignites a hidden fire.

Snowflakes twirl in an endless waltz,
Nature's chorus, without faults.
With every gust, the stories flow,
Of lives entwined in the ice and snow.

A journey beckons, step by step,
Through frozen whispers, secrets kept.
Embrace the chill, let your spirit soar,
For in the still, we're forever more.

Ethereal Tranquility

In the twilight, calm descends,
A world transformed where silence bends.
Snowflakes fall, a gentle sweep,
Lulling nature into sleep.

Stillness reigns, a sacred pause,
Life's rhythmic beat now finds its cause.
Each breath, a moment filled with grace,
Ethereal peace in this quiet space.

Stars above like diamonds gleam,
In the stillness, a fleeting dream.
Whispers of night enfold the land,
In tranquil moments, we understand.

A hush that cradles hopes and fears,
In the chill, we shed our tears.
With every sigh, the world aligns,
In the deep quiet, love entwines.

So let the night wrap you tight,
In ethereal calm, find your light.
For every heart deserves to know,
The beauty found in the falling snow.

Reflections in White Silence

In the dim light, shadows play,
White silence wraps the end of day.
Mirrored glances in the snow,
Echoes of where the heart will go.

Stillness sprawls like a canvas wide,
Nature's art, in beauty we bide.
Each breath a pause, a fleeting chance,
Captured moments in a frozen dance.

The world hushed, lost in a trance,
Glistening snowflakes, a gentle romance.
Reflections drift on the icy lake,
Whispers of dreams that gently awake.

In the embrace of the night sky's glow,
Deep in wonder, our spirits flow.
Finding solace in the frosty air,
As memories linger, tender and rare.

So when the silence calls your name,
And frozen echoes fan the flame,
Embrace the still, let your heart dance,
In reflections of life’s radiant chance.

Dreams Adrift in Frost.

In the silence, shadows creep,
Whispers of dreams, buried deep.
Frozen paths beneath the moon,
Hearts entwined, they'll find their tune.

Crystals glisten on bare trees,
A soft sigh rides the winter breeze.
Echoes dance through the still night,
Holding secrets, taking flight.

Ghostly figures glide and sway,
Lost in thoughts of yesterday.
Frosty breath in the tranquil air,
Moments linger, everywhere.

Time slows down, a gentle pause,
Nature's peace, without a cause.
Dreams adrift, they softly gleam,
Life's a fragile, fleeting dream.

Amidst the frost, we find our way,
Chasing hopes till break of day.
In every flake, a story spun,
In winter's embrace, we become one.

Whispers of Winter's Veil

Snowflakes fall like whispered breath,
Hiding warmth beneath their death.
In the quiet, secrets flow,
Wrapped in winter's gentle glow.

Stars above, their twinkle bright,
Glisten softly in the night.
Branches heavy, draped in white,
Nature's cloak, a pure delight.

Fires crackle, echo the glow,
While outside, the cold winds blow.
Inside hearts, warmth still survives,
In the stillness, hope arrives.

With every breath, the world turns slow,
Footprints marked in the soft, white snow.
Memories made beneath the skies,
In winter's hush, love never dies.

Whispers weave through the night air,
Promises made, a silent prayer.
Wrapped in dreams, we dare to dream,
In winter's embrace, we gleam.

Frosted Dreams Unfurled

Beneath the ice, dreams wait and sigh,
Frosted whispers as time glides by.
Colors muted, yet so profound,
In the stillness, magic's found.

Chill envelopes the silent ground,
Nature's voice is softly crowned.
Every flake a tale untold,
Carried forth in the winter cold.

Visions dance in shadowed light,
In the heart, warmth stirs the night.
Amidst the frost, spirit sways,
Embracing life in myriad ways.

Awakening dreams in frozen frames,
Hope ignites like fleeting flames.
From barren branches, life will bloom,
In winter’s chill, there’s room for plumes.

Frosted dreams, a fragile thread,
Binding hearts where once we tread.
In the quiet, find your way,
Through every night, into the day.

Celestial Drift

Stars cascade from heights unknown,
Celestial drift, a world alone.
In the darkness, shadows spin,
Galaxies whisper what's within.

Planetary dance, so divine,
Infinite treasures align.
Comets blaze through endless night,
Illuminating dreams in flight.

Time transcends in silent grace,
Waves of light in endless space.
Gravity pulls, yet we soar free,
Touching realms where we can see.

Nebulas bloom in colors bright,
Sculpting moments of delight.
In each drift, a wish unfurls,
Painting stories across the worlds.

Celestial beings, lost in thought,
In peaceful silence, wisdom sought.
Beyond the stars, our spirits roam,
In the cosmos, we find home.

Whispers Beneath a Frosty Canopy

In silent woods where shadows play,
The frosted breath of night turns grey.
Whispers float on icy streams,
Wrapped in winter's quiet dreams.

Branches adorned with crystals bright,
Glisten softly in pale moonlight.
Nature's breath, a frozen sigh,
Beneath the stars in a velvet sky.

Footprints vanish in purest white,
Echoes fade in the heart of night.
Where silence reigns, the world can rest,
In the arms of winter’s gentle quest.

As time stands still in silver glow,
The secrets of the forest flow.
With every breath, the magic swells,
In tales of frost the earth compels.

So listen close to nature's song,
Where whispers tell what’s right and wrong.
In this frosty, quiet land,
We find our peace, hand in hand.

The Frosted Tides

Waves of white on a restless shore,
Kissed by winter, forever more.
A symphony of ice and sea,
Dancing shadows, wild and free.

Each crest a whisper, soft and low,
Wrapped in frost, a tale to sow.
The salty air, a chill that bites,
Underneath the frostbitten lights.

Seagulls glide on frosty wings,
Carving tales of winter's strings.
The ocean breathes a cold embrace,
In its depths, a frozen grace.

Layers whisper secrets old,
In frosty tides, their stories told.
Where waves meet ice, the world aligns,
In a dance of frost, where beauty shines.

So let us walk along the line,
Where frost and tide together twine.
Each step a note in winter's hymn,
In the glow of twilight, lights grow dim.

Celestial Chills

Stars that twinkle in frosty air,
Whisper dreams beyond compare.
Celestial chills on a winter's night,
Wrap the world in soft twilight.

The moon hangs low, a silver coin,
Casting shadows fate would join.
In the hush, the cosmos sighs,
Painting dreams across the skies.

Comets trail with icy tails,
Leaving behind the ancient tales.
Galaxies swirl in a frozen dance,
Spinning secrets, a timeless chance.

In crystal nights where starlight gleams,
We wander softly through our dreams.
Each breath a wish, each heartbeat slow,
In the still, our spirits grow.

So let the chill embrace the heart,
As night and dreams shall never part.
With every star, we find our place,
In the vastness of the cosmic space.

Dreams of White Horizons

On the edge of winter's glow,
Where the silent snowflakes flow.
Dreams of white on horizons wide,
Whisper softly, the cold abide.

Fields adorned in milky lace,
Time moves slow in this sacred space.
Each flake a story, pure and bright,
In the heart of the soft starlight.

Mountains rise with ice-crowned peaks,
Guardians of the silence speaks.
In their shadows, secrets weave,
In the still, we learn to believe.

With every breath, the world unfolds,
In the winter's embrace, the heart holds.
Dreams of snow bring peace within,
In the quiet, our souls begin.

So chase the visions, let them soar,
On white horizons, forevermore.
In the chill, our hopes arise,
Painting dreams against the skies.

The Ink of Ice

Beneath the pale moonlight's glow,
The ink of ice begins to flow.
Whispers of winter softly sing,
As frozen dreams take shape in spring.

The trees wear coats of crystal lace,
Each branch a fragile, frozen trace.
In silence, shadows dance and sway,
The ink of ice holds night at bay.

A canvas wrought with chilly breath,
The artists' hands, a dance with death.
In stillness lies the world anew,
A masterpiece in shades of blue.

The dawn breaks cold, a spectral spark,
Painting warmth on shadows stark.
Yet in each drop, a story lies,
The ink of ice, where silence cries.

As twilight wraps the earth in gray,
The ink of ice will fade away.
But in our hearts, its traces stay,
A fleeting glimpse of winter's play.

A Symphony of Chill

From frosted trees, the music rings,
A symphony that winter sings.
Each note a flake that falls to ground,
In harmony, the world is found.

The wind it weaves a ghostly tune,
Beneath the watchful, glowing moon.
Each breath exhaled, a cloud of white,
In symphonies of cold delight.

The rustling leaves, a crisp refrain,
Echo the joy, the peace, the pain.
Each heartbeat beats like falling snow,
A symphony we all can know.

The icicle's drip, a metered sound,
While joints of trees twist all around.
Beneath the sky of twinkling stars,
We find our dreams where silence jars.

In silence, whispers chill the night,
The symphony is pure delight.
As winter's breath embraces all,
We dance, we sing, and heed its call.

Midnight in a White Realm

At midnight's stroke, the world stands still,
A white realm draped in winter's chill.
The stars above twinkle like snow,
As moonlight bathes the earth below.

Each snowflake whispers soft and light,
Secrets held in the deep of night.
Ghostly shadows creep and glide,
In this wonderland, we abide.

A breath of frost upon the air,
Every moment, delicate and rare.
The night's embrace, a blanket gold,
In this white realm, our dreams unfold.

The trees, like sentinels, stand tall,
Wrapped in blankets as night falls.
The hush of snow, a soft cocoon,
In midnight's grip, we find our tune.

Here in the stillness, hearts connect,
Magic lies in each moment's effect.
In this realm, our spirits soar,
Midnight whispers, forevermore.

Frosted Lanterns Above

Frosted lanterns light the night,
Glistening softly, pure delight.
They guide the way through icy paths,
As winter blooms in frosted baths.

Beneath their glow, the world transforms,
A dance of shadows that gently warms.
The crispness fills the winter air,
In this tableau, moments rare.

Each lantern’s flame a spirited song,
Carried by winds that drift along.
They twinkle with a gentle grace,
A guiding light in this frozen place.

The stars above, a silken veil,
Frosted lanterns tell our tale.
In the quiet, hearts ignite,
As winter whispers sweet and bright.

With every flicker, we find our way,
Through joy and sorrow, come what may.
The frost will fade, the lanterns sleep,
But in our hearts, the glow will keep.

A Canopy of Frosted Dreams

Underneath the silver glow,
Whispers of the night do flow.
Stars adorn the frosty air,
A shimmering tale of beauty rare.

Branches draped in icy lace,
Nature's stillness, a quiet grace.
Softly sleeps the world below,
In dreams of where the cold winds blow.

Frozen paths, a glistening sight,
Guiding souls through starry night.
Beneath the sky, so wide, so deep,
We wander slow, and softly creep.

A gentle hush wraps all around,
Magic in the quiet sound.
Each breath exhaled, a misty swirl,
In this frost-kissed, dreamlike world.

Awake we stand, yet lost in night,
Beneath this canopy of light.
In silent awe, we drink it in,
A frosted dream where we begin.

Veiled in Ice and Light

A shimmering veil of crystal bright,
Soft shadows dance in the pale moonlight.
Silent whispers in the frosty air,
Nature's artwork, beyond compare.

Glistening branches sway and bend,
In twilight's charm, all dreams extend.
Gently frozen, the world holds still,
As time drips slow, a gentle thrill.

Mirrored lakes hold secrets deep,
In icy stillness, stories keep.
Overhead, the stars convene,
In this realm of beauty serene.

A soft caress, the icy breeze,
Whispers through the ancient trees.
Veiled in magic, truth divine,
In ice and light, our dreams entwine.

As dawn appears, the crystals fade,
Yet in our hearts, the memories stayed.
A fleeting glimpse of winter's grace,
In the quiet, sacred space.

Translucent Beauty Above

A sky of blue with silver threads,
Translucent light where beauty spreads.
Clouds like whispers float on high,
Painting dreams across the sky.

Fragments of the sun cascade,
In the air, a soft parade.
Illuminating all in sight,
The world awakened, pure delight.

Gleams of hope in every ray,
Calling forth the dawn of day.
In this dance of light and shade,
Nature's canvas, hand displayed.

The whispers of the wind take flight,
Carrying wishes through the light.
A serenade of warmth and grace,
In translucent beauty, we embrace.

With each fleeting moment's glance,
We find ourselves in nature's dance.
Above us shines the radiant glow,
A reminder of the love we know.

The Crystal Dome

Within a dome of sparkling light,
I stand awed by the winter night.
Each flake a gem, each breath a song,
In this crystal world where I belong.

The stars convene in a silent choir,
Filling hearts with a quiet fire.
A soft glow resonates around,
Lost in the beauty, I'm spellbound.

Frosted paths and glimmering streams,
Guiding us through a land of dreams.
Nature wrapped in a tender embrace,
In the crystal dome, time finds its place.

Across the sky, the moonlight weaves,
Secrets held in the frosty leaves.
Each moment, a treasure, softly shown,
In this special realm, we have grown.

Awakened spirits in the night,
Drawn together by the softest light.
In the crystal dome, hearts align,
Forever cherished, forever mine.

Aurora in the Cold

Dancing lights in the frosty air,
Colors swirl, with magic to share.
Whispers of night, so gentle and bright,
Embraced by the beauty of winter's delight.

Stars as witnesses, silent and wise,
Awakening dreams under twilight skies.
Nature's canvas, a wondrous display,
Beneath the vast heavens, the cold fades away.

Shadows linger where silence remains,
Echoes of warmth in snow-laden plains.
Each breath a promise, each moment a song,
In the heart of the cold, where wonders belong.

The chill wraps around like a tender embrace,
Guiding the night's soft and tranquil pace.
Eager hearts chase the shimmering glow,
As auroras dance in a world draped in snow.

A fleeting spectacle, yet timeless it seems,
Awakening the world to magical dreams.
With every flicker, a story is told,
In the heart of the winter, where auroras unfold.

Echoes of a Quiet Storm

Whispers of winds, a delicate sound,
Rumbles of thunder, a soft echo found.
Each droplet falls with a dancer's grace,
In the realm of stillness, time finds its place.

Trees sway gently, in rhythm, they breathe,
Nature's enchantment, a woven sheath.
Lightning flickers, revealing the night,
In the cradle of shadows, hidden delight.

Clouds gather close, a blanket of grey,
Holding the magic in a silvery play.
Moments suspended, a hush fills the air,
Heartbeats the only sound, a calm, sweet despair.

Raindrops like whispers, on rooftops they sigh,
Creating a symphony, where dreams linger high.
Echoes of twilight, a story unfolds,
In the embrace of the night, a warmth that consoles.

And when storms fade, revealing pure light,
The world emerges, fresh from the night.
Every blade of grass glistens in tune,
Beneath the soft glow of the silvery moon.

Frosty Whispers

In quiet corners, the frost gently creeps,
Whispers of winter, where silent snow sleeps.
Each crystal a secret, each flake a tale,
Carved by the winds, soft as a veil.

Branches adorned in delicate lace,
Nature's artwork, frozen in grace.
Gentle and serene, the world slows its pace,
In the heart of the stillness, a warm embrace.

Echoes of laughter in the cold crisp air,
Frolicking children with not a care.
Snowflakes like kisses that dance on the ground,
In this winter wonderland, joy can be found.

Moonlight cascades on the blanket of white,
Guiding the dreams that slip through the night.
Each breath a whisper, soft and profound,
In the realm where magic and chill can be found.

As dawn brings the glow, the frost slowly fades,
But echoes of beauty linger in glades.
Nature's soft promise, in white it persists,
Frosty whispers that linger in mists.

Veils of Winter's Night

Veils of winter, soft and serene,
Cloak the world in a silvery sheen.
Stars twinkle shyly, hidden from view,
In the embrace of the night, dreams come true.

The moon casts shadows, long and deep,
Secrets are stirred, as silence does seep.
Frosted branches sway, breath of a chill,
Whispers of winter, enchanting and still.

Footsteps muffled on pathways of snow,
Each one a story, where memories flow.
In the still of the dark, the heart finds its way,
Guided by starlight, where magic holds sway.

A spark of warmth in a world dressed in white,
In the quiet of night, love takes to flight.
Moments linger long, wrapped in delight,
In the veils of winter, everything feels right.

As dawn approaches with a soft, golden hue,
Nature awakens, a beautiful view.
But deep in the soul, the night shall remain,
Veils of winter's magic, never in vain.

When the Skies Whisper Cold

Whispers weave through the trees,
Chilling breath of winter's ease.
Bare branches tremble, hush of night,
Stars twinkle in frosty light.

Footsteps crunch on crisp, white ground,
Echoes of silence, all around.
Moonlight spills like silver tears,
Cloaked in shadows, it appears.

Frosted air, a biting kiss,
Each gust carries a sense of bliss.
Nature sleeps under the quilt,
Of snowflakes that gently wilt.

Glimmers dance in twilight's glow,
Beneath the stars, dreams gently flow.
In the quiet, hearts align,
Whispers grow, the stars entwine.

In the stillness, hope ignites,
In winter's breath, new dreams take flight.
As skies whisper their secrets bold,
Embrace the night, let stories unfold.

Iridescence in a Frozen Realm

Colors shimmer on ice so clear,
Whispers of magic linger near.
Frozen waves in a dazzling hue,
Nature's canvas, fresh and new.

Crisp morning air, a pastel glow,
Reflecting treasures hidden below.
With each breath, the world stands still,
In this realm of frost and chill.

Sunlight kisses the glistening space,
Creating sparkles that softly grace.
A winter's tale, gently told,
In hues of lavender and gold.

Iridescence cloaks the land,
A fleeting moment, so grand.
In the stillness, beauty gleams,
Awakening forgotten dreams.

In this frozen realm, we wander,
Entranced by beauty, lost in wonder.
Embrace the chill, let spirits soar,
In nature's art, we crave for more.

Nightfall's Tender Touch

As day surrenders to twilight's grace,
Nightfall comes with a soft embrace.
Stars awaken, bright as dreams,
Whispers echo in silver beams.

Cool shadows stretch across the land,
Greeting the dark with a gentle hand.
The moon rises, pure and bright,
Guiding souls through the velvet night.

In the distance, an owl calls,
Nature listens as silence falls.
Soft winds carry secrets untold,
Comfort found in the night so bold.

Each star a promise hanging high,
A canvas splashed across the sky.
In the darkness, there's peace to find,
A tender touch, the heart unwind.

So let the night enfold your heart,
In stillness, know we are a part.
Of dreams that dance in moonlight's glow,
In nightfall's touch, we come to know.

The Stillness of Winter's Embrace

In a blanket of white, the world holds still,
Winter’s breath is a gentle thrill.
The trees stand tall in tranquil grace,
Nature’s spirit, a warm embrace.

Snowflakes twirl like whispered sighs,
Filling the earth beneath the skies.
Footprints fade in the morning light,
As dreams awaken, soft and bright.

Crisp air bites, yet hearts are warm,
Surrounded by winter's calming charm.
Each moment lingers, a quiet pause,
In stillness, we find our cause.

The world transforms, a stunning sight,
In winter's grasp, all feels right.
Time bends slow, as shadows play,
In the stillness of the winter’s sway.

So breathe it in, this serene space,
Let the chill invite your grace.
In winter’s arms, we've found our place,
In stillness, love leaves its trace.

Winter's Whispered Embrace

In twilight's hush, the snowflakes fall,
A silent dance, they blanket all.
The world adorned in frosted grace,
Winter whispers, a soft embrace.

Bare branches stretch, like fingers cold,
Wrapped in white, their secrets told.
The air is crisp, with whispers near,
Nature's lullaby, sweet and clear.

Footprints trace a tale of old,
With every step, a story unfolds.
The hearth glows warm, a heart's delight,
In winter's arms, we find our light.

Stars emerge in the velvet skies,
Each one a dream, where hope never dies.
We gather close, with laughter and cheer,
In winter's whisper, we hold dear.

So let the cold winds gently blow,
For in this chill, our spirits grow.
From icy breath, the warmth will rise,
In winter's hush, our love complies.

Crystal Canopy Dreams

Underneath the sky's vast dome,
A crystal canopy we call home.
Stars twinkle like diamonds at night,
Guiding our dreams in soft moonlight.

Whispers of winds through the trees,
Nature's symphony, a gentle breeze.
Leaves shimmer with the morning dew,
Each glint a story, forgotten but true.

Clouds drift softly in shades of white,
Painting the dawn with hues of light.
Colors bloom in the arms of spring,
A tapestry made, where joy will sing.

With each new day, the sun will rise,
Casting warmth upon our skies.
In every moment, a chance to gleam,
Awake to the world, in a crystal dream.

So let us wander, here and there,
In this expanse, with love to share.
Beneath the canopy, hearts ignite,
In dreams so vivid, pure and bright.

Beneath the Silent Blanket

A world hushed under winter’s embrace,
Beneath the silent, snowy lace.
Each flake a whisper, soft and light,
Covering earth, a starry night.

Branches bow with a frosty crown,
Nature sleeps in a cozy gown.
The moon peeks down, a watchful eye,
While dreams unfold in the quiet sky.

Footsteps muffled by nature's quilt,
In this stillness, all worries wilt.
Moments frozen in time's gentle hold,
Stories of ages quietly told.

Fires crackle, casting a glow,
While outside, the harsh winds blow.
Yet in our hearts, warmth stays alive,
In winter's blanket, our hopes will thrive.

So linger here, let time drift slow,
In this serene, enchanted show.
Together we find, ‘neath winter's spell,
A sanctuary, where all is well.

Frosted Horizons Unveiled

As dawn breaks forth, in silver hue,
Frosted horizons come into view.
Nature's canvas, a sparkling scene,
Awakening dreams, serene and clean.

Mountains clad in a cloak of white,
Glinting jewels in the soft sunlight.
The rivers whisper, glacial and clear,
In this frosty realm, we hold dear.

Footsteps crunch on the icy ground,
Echoes of joy in their joyous sound.
Snowflakes spin, a delicate waltz,
In winter's grip, we find no faults.

Clouds drift lazily, a soft parade,
Casting shadows, nature's charade.
As colors bloom, the world awakes,
In frosted hues, our spirits break.

So let us dance through winter's chill,
Embrace the beauty, savor the thrill.
For in each breath, we find our way,
Through frosted horizons, come what may.

A Spectrum of Chill

In the quiet of the dawn,
A blanket of frost does dawn.
Colors shift in icy breath,
Chill whispers of winter's depth.

Trees don coats of shimmering white,
Branches dance in morning light.
The sky blushes deep and pale,
Soft as stories lost in tale.

Footprints crunch on frozen ground,
Silence sings without a sound.
Nature sleeps in crystal dreams,
A world composed of silver gleams.

Each note of frost tells a tale,
Winds weave spells that never fail.
Echoes of the coldest nights,
Warmth in waiting; hope ignites.

As the sun bows to the moon,
Stillness cradles nature's tune.
In this spectrum, colors blend,
Winter's canvas knows no end.

The Beauty of White Horizons

A world dressed in snowy lace,
Horizon stretches, an endless space.
Whispers of peace in every flake,
Soft like dreams that silence makes.

Mountains raised in splendor bright,
Tucked beneath the starlit night.
Each ridge glows with purest white,
Nature wrapped in gentle light.

Footsteps echo on the trail,
A winter's peace, a silent tale.
Immersed in beauty, hearts unwind,
The frosted air, a balm for mind.

Branches sag with crystal weights,
The beauty of winter never waits.
Every shadow paints a scene,
As if the world wears a pristine sheen.

In this beauty, silence roams,
Each breath a promise; winter's homes.
Horizons bright with snowy dreams,
Serenity flows in shimmering streams.

Starlit Frost on Pine

Pines adorned with frosty crowns,
Stand like sentinels in gowns.
Twinkling stars adorn the night,
Nature cradled in soft light.

Whispers float on chilly air,
Echoes dance without a care.
Beneath the trees, the blanket sprawls,
Winter's grace in silent calls.

Moonlight kisses icy tips,
As the world in wonder sips.
Frosty glitter twirls and weaves,
Stories told by frosted leaves.

Boughs sway gently in the breeze,
Carrying secrets with such ease.
Nature hums a soothing song,
In this realm where hearts belong.

Every corner, a quiet glow,
Winter's magic, soft and slow.
Starlit frost on ancient pine,
An enchanted night, wholly divine.

Winter's Secret Symphony

A hush falls over silent fields,
As winter's breath gently yields.
Nature's notes in crisp, cool air,
A soft melody everywhere.

Chiming sleigh bells in the night,
Echo through the moon's soft light.
Each flake dances, twirls in glee,
Nature sings its lullaby, free.

Icicles hang like crystal gems,
Nature plays on frosted stems.
Whispers of the world, anew,
Winter's secrets, shared with you.

Breezes carry tales of old,
Fables wrapped in gleaming gold.
The woods embrace the chilling breeze,
As winter's song flows with such ease.

In the quiet, hearts awake,
To the sounds the stillness makes.
Each note a reason to believe,
In winter's love, we find reprieve.

Frost-kissed Reverie

In the morning glow of light,
White crystals shine, a lovely sight.
Each breath hangs, a misty lace,
Nature smiles, in frosty grace.

Beneath the trees, a silent hush,
Footprints left in a gentle crush.
Whispers linger, soft and bright,
In this world, all feels just right.

Sparkling stars in the night air,
Winter's charm, beyond compare.
Dreams unfold in silver hue,
A frosted dawn feels fresh and new.

Through the woods, a fleeting glance,
Frozen streams in a twilight dance.
Echoes of a soft refrain,
Waltzing with the crystal rain.

With every breath, a story spun,
Wrapped in warmth, when day is done.
Frost-kissed moments, pure and rare,
In this reverie, we're almost there.

Where Time Stands Still in White

When the world is draped in snow,
Time seems slow, a gentle flow.
Footsteps pause on frozen ground,
Here, a quiet peace is found.

Trees adorned in icy gowns,
Silence reigns, no worldly sounds.
Each flake falls with purpose true,
Wrapping earth in a chilly blue.

Crystalline dreams in a winter light,
Magic weaves through the soft night.
Under starlit skies, our hearts,
Find the solace that winter imparts.

The horizon glows, a fleeting sight,
Dawn breaks softly, igniting light.
Within this stillness, souls can heal,
In white embraces, we find what's real.

Let the snowflakes settle down,
In this realm, wear joy like a crown.
Where time pauses, hearts take flight,
In the wonder of purest white.

The Shimmering Veil of Evenings

As the day slips into dreams,
Softly fades the sunlight's beams.
Twilight whispers, secrets shared,
The night air, calm and unprepared.

Stars awaken, with a gentle glow,
In the darkness, day’s last show.
Frost gathers on the window's pane,
Locking warmth with winter’s chain.

Moonlight dances on the snow,
Casting shadows, silvery flow.
Each heartbeat echoes with delight,
In the shimmering veil of night.

Chill winds carry tales of old,
Once forgotten, now retold.
Where dreams entwine, and spirits soar,
The evening's grace opens every door.

In this hour, we pause to see,
Nature's magic, wild and free.
Wrapped in night’s enchanting spell,
In the shimmering, we dwell.

Celestial Dreams in Frost

Under a night, so deeply vast,
Stars emerge, a cosmic cast.
Frosty breezes twirl and bite,
Yet warmth blooms in pure delight.

Crystals gleam, like wishes spun,
In the silence, dreams begun.
Celestial mysteries swirl and twirl,
In this magic, hearts unfurl.

Golden lights among the pines,
Frost-kissed whispers, soft designs.
Pale moon arcs in skies so high,
Guiding souls as they pass by.

Moments linger, suspended time,
In frost's embrace, we find our rhyme.
Every breath, a hymn to night,
In the dark, our spirits unite.

Celestial realms, where we belong,
In the chill, we feel so strong.
Dreams of frost and stars collide,
In this wonder, we reside.

www.ingramcontent.com/pod-product-compliance
Ingram Content Group UK Ltd.
Pitfield, Milton Keynes, MK11 3LW, UK
UKHW031941151224
452382UK00006B/198

9 789916 793183